Brother of the Bride

Palewell Press

Brother of the Bride
shopping for my sister's wedding dress

Joseph Kaifala

Brother of the Bride – shopping for my sister's wedding dress

First edition 2022 from Palewell Press, www.palewellpress.co.uk

Printed and bound in the UK

ISBN 978-1-911587-66-8

All Rights Reserved. Copyright © 2022 Joseph Kaifala. No part of this publication may be reproduced or transmitted in any form or by any means, without permission in writing from the author. The right of Joseph Kaifala to be identified as the author of this work has been asserted by him in accordance with the Copyright, Designs and Patents Act 1988

The front and back cover images are Copyright © 2022 Joseph Kaifala

The cover design is Copyright © 2022 Camilla Reeve

A CIP catalogue record for this title is available from the British Library.

Acknowledgements

I am grateful to my friend Alicia Wells Day for all her support.

I thank my sister Hawa Kaifala-Samba and her husband Augustine Samba. Special thanks to my brothers, Francis Ben Kaifala, Sahr Kendema, Musa Adams Tongi, Kaifala Tongi, Jr., Ben Kaifala, John Kettor and Mathew Kaifala. To my sisters, Amie Camara, Watta and Mariata Sandouno, Sia Rose Tolno, Sia Tolno, Doris Jamiru, Francess Lamin, and Dandora Tongi.

Thank you to Josephine Kamara, Nadia Assad, Nyangah Rogers-Wright, Affia Mackawe Bertin, Binta Umu Jalloh, Aminata Kamara, Victoria Ballah, Mary J.B. Kamara, Isata George-Sankoh, Massah E.N. Bockarie, Isha Morgan-Conteh, Haja Umu Jalloh, Kaata Komeh Minah, Lindsay Agatha Sesay and Haja Sowa, including Zainab O. Sheriff, Naasu Fofanah, Haja Isatu Bah, Yakama Manty Jones, Diaka Selena Koroma, Yeiwah Kaindaneh and Sawa Kamara.

To Chernor Bah and Aissatou Mila, Sian Lord-Baptiste, Hawa O. Brima, Eartha Burke, Rosa Bransky, Augustine Brima, Nicky Coker, Kamila Janczyk, Swatee Deepak, and Makmid Kamara.

Thank you to Sylvia Arthur, Seth Avusuglo, Adachukwu Onwudiwe, Soonest Nathaniel, Akumbu Uche and Mofiyinfoluwa Okupe. My team, Wuya S. Kallon, Madonna L. Garber and Rugiatu J. Kamara. Special thanks to Camilla Reeve and Palewell Press.

Dedication

To Michael Steven Marx and Catherine Golden

Contents

Foreword by Alicia Wells Day	1
I	7
II	10
III	16
IV	22
V	25
VI	31
VII	42
VIII	45
IX	49
X	53
XI	60
XII	69
XIII	75
XIV	84
XV	92
Joseph Kaifala - Biography	96

Foreword by Alicia Wells Day

I met Joseph during my sophomore year at Skidmore College. We were part of the Residential Life staff for McClellan Hall. Often, throughout the semester, I would return to my dorm room from completing rounds and find Joseph curled up on my floor asleep. I was a Psychology major, but I took enough classes in the Education and English departments to qualify for a minor in both. After Skidmore, I obtained an MA in Special Education. In 2012, I went to Sierra Leone to work with Joseph on a few projects he was just starting while he was finishing his law degree at Vermont Law School. Then in 2019, I completed a second MA in Behavior Analysis and returned to visit Joseph and provided some professional development for classroom management strategies to the teachers of the school, for which we had helped to clear land in 2012.

In college, some residents had the assumption that Joseph was a Casanova. Having spent a significant amount of time in his dorm room, I can assure you that he was not. Joseph's dorm room was bare compared to other dorm rooms. He didn't even have a pillow. His room was littered with notebooks, stacks of books, empty dirty coffee mugs, beer cans, a selection of movies, and apple cores in, and out, of the trash. When my friends heard that I was getting to know Joseph they warned me about this "reputation." I don't know where it came from. Joseph is a well-spoken, but quiet person. He certainly liked to get together with his friends and party, but he could also very easily be found in a quiet corner of these parties with a beer in hand, debating whatever current event was brought up. He took his academics seriously and took multiple independent studies, which focused on various writings or films he was interested in making, ranging from the importance of the Poda-Poda (a minivan used for public transportation) to the Sierra Leonean economy, and female genital mutilation. Over coffee, or beer and the occasional game of scrabble, I got to know that Joseph was someone who valued his relationships with others. He took his role in the world seriously and would use the opportunities he had to make the world a better place.

As finals concluded and his trip home for the holidays and his older sister's wedding approached, Joseph sent me a message asking if I would drive him to Albany to get a dress from David's Bridal. I vaguely recall that he also suggested the option of picking one up at the airport. I told him this was not a good plan. I had one more final, but I thought it was in the evening, so I agreed to take him to Albany as long as he helped me dig out my minivan from whatever snow drift it was buried in.

We arrived at the store without an appointment, something neither of us realized we needed, but the middle of winter isn't really a wedding season in the US, so we were able to get an associate to help us. At first, the woman assumed I was the bride. I hurriedly explained that I was not. Then she looked at Joseph and asked if he were the bride. He just doubled over in laughter, leaving me to explain the situation. We established that neither of us were the bride and that we would need a wedding dress that day for Joseph to take with him to Sierra Leone.

This poor saleswoman. Now, having been a bride myself, I understand more of what this woman went through with the two of us. The only thing close to wedding dress shopping I had ever done was buying a prom dress at Macy's. When I purchased my own wedding dress, I went to three different stores before finding a dress that wasn't quite what I was looking for, but with alterations, would be perfect. This was months before my actual wedding date. I then had three fittings where the seamstress added straps, changed the neckline, hemmed the dress, and added a bustle. This is what the saleswoman was assuming would happen for this wedding, because that's what the process is in the US. It was no wonder she was appalled when we told her the bride wouldn't be trying on the dress before we took it with us and that she wasn't even in the US.

All Joseph brought with him to the store was his sister's measurements - a series of numbers without any units. Meaning they were mostly useless, but we guessed and decided larger would be better. You can't create fabric, but dresses can be taken in. As we wandered the racks of dresses that were available that day to be taken off the rack, Joseph asked about my final. I told him it was for my Environmental Literature class, a class I was taking with his advisor, Professor Marx. As I recall, Joseph was quite casual when he mentioned that a mutual friend, also in my class, had the final that morning. At this point I was not casual. I took my grades seriously and had no idea how missing a final exam would affect my grade and my relationship with the professor. Joseph assured me that Professor Marx knew of his dilemma with the dress and would look favourably on me when Joseph helped to explain what happened. I wanted to drop everything and return to campus as quickly as possible to explain everything, but Joseph in his calming way pointed out that I would have missed the final with or without the trip, given I was convinced it was in the evening, and it was probably better that we returned to campus having succeeded with Joseph's task so that Professor Marx would see what a wonderful friend I was and be more willing to be lenient.

Joseph found a dress that he liked on a final sale rack. And we had to explain once again that his sister would not be coming in to try the dress. I convinced the woman helping us that all would be fine in West Africa where the wedding was being held because Joseph's mother is a seamstress and could alter the dress herself. Pacified that the dress would be safe after we removed it from the store, we started looking at undergarments, and it was Joseph's turn to blush. I took over understanding at least a bit about what would be needed to provide the structure necessary to hold the dress away from the bride's legs and keep her comfortable and picked out a bunch of crinoline that would do the trick.

Then there was a veil. Neither of us knew what to do with a veil and I knew that I never wanted to wear one! But given that Joseph needed a model, I was sacrificed. The associate showed Joseph how the comb sat in my hair and then pulled the front piece over my face and pushed it back again to show how it would work. I was horrified and uncomfortable the entire time. I still believe Joseph drew out the process to amuse himself with my suffering. With a dress in the garment bag and another bag of crinoline along with a few other dresses for cousins and Joseph's other sisters, we climbed back into the van to return to campus.

Joseph walked with me to Professor Marx's office. I remember apologizing profusely for missing the final and then letting Joseph tell the story. Looking back, I don't even remember what the outcome was. Just that I at least passed the class.

My friendship with Joseph has been full of beer, coffee, and discussions of problems affecting the world as we see it and how to address them. Joseph is one of the few people I know who sees a problem in the world and sets out to solve that problem. Many of us talk about what needs to be done to change things for the better but then we become caught up in our own lives and therefore never do much to help make these solutions reality. Joseph sees practical solutions to big problems and acts.

I have taken two trips to Sierra Leone. The first trip, we helped Joseph document the stories of people who survived the civil war including child soldiers and amputees who told heart wrenching stories of violence and loss. We also bought and began clearing land for what is now the Sengbe Pieh Academy, a school for girls which provides free education to girls of the community. During my second trip I met these girls and worked with their teachers to support them in their educational practices.

I remain a great supporter of Joseph's work with the Center for Memory and Reparations and the Jeneba Project.

Thank you, Alicia Wells Day

I

I have always found wedding ceremonies interesting. Interesting, from the comfort of a guest's chair, where my mind meanders from a sometimes tearful, romantic ceremony, to what food and drinks might be at the reception. Behind spectacular décors, nice clothes, beautiful speeches, a fine cake that should never be eaten, and a wonderful party, lie disagreements, family disputes, tears, stress and moments of doubt — that is, whether one should marry or not marry. I could quote credible evidence that humans are not monogamist, but that would only be in vain, because there is even more overwhelming evidence against polygamy. But in extreme cases, the question of whether one should marry or not could lead to cold feet – so frozen that the individual doesn't even make it to the altar. But before I comment on this matter any further, here is a disclaimer: I have never been married. So, this conclusion is the convenient point of view of a bachelor. This is not to say that there are no marriages where all parties are joyful from inception to eternity, where only death doth part, but many marriages must first jump various hurdles, because marriage is a merger and people are often reluctant to share, even when they are deeply in love.

The part about stress and moments of doubt I actually heard from married friends — some of whom confessed to brief moments when they wanted to disappear from the altar. The Hamlet conundrum of "To be or not to be" is a human dilemma that confronts us in the face of life-transforming choices. One knows one should, but one doubts that one could. Marriage is clearly a union, and in every union each party surrenders something for the benefit of the whole. Time and time again we've heard a Reverend Father quote these words from the Bible: `For this cause shall a man leave his father and mother, and shall be joined unto his wife, and the two shall be one flesh`. Nowadays, it appears it is a woman who is expected to leave her father and mother for the cause of marriage – this is why it is a man who traditionally asks for a woman's hand in marriage. Increasing global acceptance of gay marriage is presenting a serious challenge for many African countries where homosexuality remains illegal. In any event, standing at the altar, in the presence of God and man (depending on your belief or lack thereof), when you take the other and the other takes you under oath, individual freedom is diminished on both sides. The two human beings become one flesh in separate bodies.

I was single and a junior at Skidmore College, in upstate New York, when my sister decided to marry. I could not have foreseen that I would assume one of the biggest responsibilities of my older sister's wedding — that is, buying her wedding dress. Among the many brotherly roles I have been expected to play, I had not imagined that I would be frantically searching stores, after a New York snow blizzard in December 2007, shopping for a wedding dress for my older sister. The weight of this responsibility is felt when one learns that at this point in my life I only knew three units of measurement for clothes: small, medium and large. Now, I was about to buy a wedding dress for a woman I had not seen in almost two years.

II

I have two biological sisters: Hawa and Amie. Hawa is the oldest and Amie is the youngest of the four of us. My younger brother Francis and I are in the middle of these two girls. My mother, Tewa, always emphasized our role of protecting the girls, but it was never clear to me that dressing my sisters for marriage would be one of those brotherly roles my mother expected of me and Francis. In reality, I never gave any consideration to the thought of my sisters leaving their father, mother and brothers, for marriage. I saw other girls marry, of course, but that could never be my sisters, I believed as a child.

I love my sisters dearly and I would do anything for them, but playing bridesmaid was something I did not take seriously until it dawned on me that it was not a joking matter. When I came to college in the US, Francis remained in Freetown, Hawa and my mother stayed as refugees in Kissidougou, Guinea, and Amie lived with my aunt Mama Yawa in Conakry. We called each other from time to time for updates and whatever support was needed in our lives.

In 2007, Hawa was engaged to a young man called Augustine. My uncle, Docteur Sandouno, Mama Yawa's husband, called from Conakry to inform me that a man had appeared for Hawa. Since the death of my father, Docteur Sandouno stepped in when we needed a father. Augustine had come to "show face." In Sierra Leonean parlance, this simply means that my sister had a suitor and he had come to declare his intention to marry her. This is when the man literally shows his face to the girl's parents – emerging from the obscurity of secret desires to boldly profess his love in the presence of the girl's family. In a traditional Sierra Leonean setting, one does not go up a mountain and pull out a ring, hoping the girl says yes. One goes to the girl's father and says I have seen a beautiful flower in your garden and I want to pluck it. You pluck the flower only with the father's permission.

In other situations, the marriage is arranged by two families who believe their children would make a great couple, usually for pragmatic reasons unrelated to love. Back in the day, a bachelor of my age would have already received a wife, nurtured and tamed by my parents in collusion with the girl's parents. Standards of duty and respect often prevented the couple from rejecting the arrangement. These days, by the time the suitor shows up to ask for permission to pluck a flower from his future father-in-law's garden, the rose and ivy had already commingled.

My family needed my approval before my sister could marry. Had my father been alive, that would have been his lot, but our old man died when we first entered Guinea in 1994 as refugees. I had taken his place by virtue of patriarchal succession rules. When a father dies, his oldest son becomes the new head of the family, no matter his age or rank among his siblings. This rule sometimes becomes the crux of the *wahala*, problem, between many African mothers-in-law and daughters-in-law who keep giving birth to girls. Some mothers-in-law react as though their daughters-in-law are making deliberate choices not to give birth to boys. Many of our African mothers are pedantic guardians of the very patriarchal systems that once abused them, often compelling their daughters to accept the status quo, which feeds a vicious circle of discrimination and gender inequality. I knew Augustine, my future brother-in-law. He had been dating Hawa even before I left Sierra Leone in 2002 to attend the Red Cross Nordic United World College in Norway. Though I did not know him then, Augustine and I were stuck behind rebel lines during the Liberian civil war. His father and mine viewed each other as brothers. Augustine is a nice guy. I gave my approval without hesitation, plus Hawa was already with him and she knew him better – this was a case of the rose and the ivy already commingling.

"He is a good man; let them marry." I told my uncle on the phone.

My approval may have been granted while I was nursing one of those undergraduate hangovers of my junior year. The first two years of college is usually a time of exploration and self-definition. The third year is when, in my experience, one becomes a collegian, a citizen of one's learning space. In the senior year, this is even more pronounced because whatever the matter, one has been there, done that. One has war stories to tell freshmen and experiences to share. I spent most of my junior and senior years with my friend Peter Brock who was one of the Vice Presidents of the Skidmore College International Affairs Club. I was the President. Peter and I bonded over our love for beer and the Symposium — a Socratic intellectual drinking party. This means I spent many late nights drinking and debating global issues with Peter and other friends.

I sometimes left Peter's place in Scribner village, the Skidmore sophomore quarters, or Northwoods, the newly constructed student housing for upper-class students, and returned to McClellan, the campus dormitory where I was a Residential Assistant, very early in the morning. Calls from home usually came in as soon as I hit the sack because of the five hour time difference between New York and Freetown, Conakry, and Monrovia. I always tried to sound better than I actually felt when my mother called. She was prone to assume the worst whenever she heard even a minor hoarse in my voice. "Are you sick? Did you eat today? You are not well?"

My mother is well aware that I can take care of myself. Many years ago, after my father died, which left her with four children to raise in a refugee camp, we learned to survive on almost anything, anywhere and under any circumstance. She raised us to persevere even when perseverance seems impossible. So even from West Africa, she knew I could thrive, but what would a mother do without asking? And so she did.

"*Ar de du fayn.*" I am doing alright. I answered in Krio.

I have always felt my mother's faith in me. She gave me the name "Joseph" not only because that was her father's name; she has reverence for three Josephs in the Bible: Joseph, the Father of Christ; Joseph of Arimathea; Joseph, the Dreamer or the Brother of Benjamin. She called me these names depending on what she expected of me on any given occasion. Joseph, the Father of Christ, was expected to be trusting, loving and caring. Joseph of Arimathea was required to be generous to others. This Joseph was the one who undertook the responsibility of Jesus' burial. It is recorded that the tomb where Jesus was buried belonged to him. Many Christians know the story of "Joseph the Dreamer or Brother of Benjamin" who was one of the Twelve Sons of Jacob. This is the Joseph, interestingly, my mother loved more than the others. This parental favouritism was one of the reasons Joseph's brothers sold him into slavery. My mother once sewed a Coat of Many Colors for me from leftover fabrics from her tailor shop. To probably avoid repeating the same situation that led to the fate of her beloved Joseph, the Dreamer, she made one for Francis too. I loved my Coat of Many Colors and I wore it for many years, because as mothers often do, it was sewn large so I could grow into it.

Whenever I listen to Dolly Parton's *Coat of Many Colors*, I think of my mother. In those days we, too, had no money and my mother was dealing with the grief of losing her beloved husband, but I felt handsome and loved in my Coat of Many Colors.

III

When I approved Hawa's betrothal and my uncle hung up the phone, she called to confirm her intent to marry. After a moment of laughter through which we made fun of eccentric family members and discussed family news, Hawa got to the point of informing me that she was getting married.

"*Ar de mared.*" I am getting married, she said in a dull voice, as if to bring a sudden end to our silly old ways.

I felt a little tinge of sadness before she burst out laughing on the other end of the phone line.

I started to giggle, nervously. We do this often. My sister laughs and I feel the contagion. But unlike other times, this moment of laughter was brief. There was a sudden silence.

"Hello?"

"Hello?" I shouted into the receiver.

Sudden silences across international phone lines were not unusual immediately after the 9/11 terrorist attacks on the US. Either one used the wrong word and a government spyware intercepted the conversation or it was just another bad day for international calls. Nothing was wrong on this occasion. My sister had simply paused to ask a major favor that apparently required a moment of silence. This is what she does when she wants to draw a line between our silliness and a serious matter that requires my full attention. It is her way of indicating that playtime is over and she is about to tell me something serious.

Hawa unveiled her main reason for calling that night. Despite our friendship, she is often shy when asking me for a favor. I have to read her expressions and basically force her to ask. She eventually asks, but the request is usually succeeded by the phrase, *if yu abul du am* – if you can do it. However, the request on that memorable day was authoritative. I guess when one is making the mother of all requests, one practices assertiveness, lest it is taken for an ordinary request. She was transmitting her seriousness across the phone line.

"*Ar wan mek yu buy me yawo klos na Amerika.*" I want you to buy my wedding dress in America.

Before I could process the information, she went on describing her favorite shape, style, color, where she had seen it, who was wearing it, etc. I must confess, all that information went right through one ear and out the other. Somewhere in that jibber-jabber, she mentioned size and provided a rationale for why she particularly wanted me to buy her wedding dress in the US. I was glad she asked for help, but the weight of my responsibility had not yet dawned on me. Had I foreseen the intricacies of purchasing a wedding dress in the US, I would have listened well, especially to the part regarding size.

Without a new wedding dress Hawa would have had to rent one from a recycled bridal gown store. There is nothing wrong with this idea — recycling dresses people expect to wear once in a lifetime – forever after. But most of the dresses available for rent in Kissidougou had been worn by so many brides, they were closer to brown than to the white they used to be. Hawa would never wear a decolorated dress, especially not on a special occasion like her wedding day. My mother is a seamstress and my sisters grew up getting fashionably dressed for church.

Hawa could certainly not obtain a new wedding dress in Kissidougou because many people in that part of Guinea are Muslims, and the market for wedding dresses is limited, because Muslims are just happy getting married in traditional attires. Hawa was never going to find a proper Christian wedding dress in that area. We lost everything in the Sierra Leonean civil war and became refugees, but there are certain standards my mother, even during the difficulties created by the war and refugee life, was unwilling to lower. We are Catholics and holy matrimony is a sacrament. It does not matter whether her children remain practicing Catholics as long as they respect the sacraments. I am the challenger of religion, but even yours truly, "Martin Luther," zips it when mother is home. My mother matters to me more than my views on religion.

My mother meticulously preserved her wedding dress and other items for her two daughters, but we lost all those things in the war. I still remember when I would watch my mother open her silver trunk in Pendembu, our hometown in Sierra Leone, to lend her bridal accessories to one young woman or another who was getting married. My mother could have made a beautiful dress for Hawa like she did for my stepsister Doris when she got married not long after we got to Guinea as refugees, but Hawa wanted a wedding dress from the US, and so she turned to her younger brother – the one person who knew nothing about wedding regalia.

Perhaps it is because we were here before our two siblings, Francis and Amie, Hawa and I have always connected better. When we were children, she used to tickle me for long periods to make me laugh so my dimples would show. She still finds my double dimples cute. I remember days when she made me laugh so hard that I almost lost my breath. Hawa is also the only one in my family who honestly believes that I am a great dancer – everyone else says I dance like I don't hear the music.

Before the war, Hawa lived with my cousin Jeneba and her husband, Francis Foday, in Kenema, Sierra Leone. I moved to Liberia to live with my father. I only saw Hawa during holidays when we returned to Pendembu. Each night we fought for the privilege to sleep in our grandmother Mama Jeneba's bed. We often ended up falling asleep behind Mama Jeneba, after hours of wrestling for space and proximity to grandma. I used to laugh so hard that Mama Jeneba would complain that Hawa was going to break my rib. I grew up wondering how laughter could ever break anyone's rib.

When the Sierra Leonean civil war started in 1991, Jeneba was in Pendembu, cut off from Kenema as rebels took the highway between Pendembu and Kenema. We did not see Hawa again until 1994 when we ended up in Guinea as refugees. My relationship with Hawa was no longer the same. I had become a witness to two bloody wars I did not fully understand and the chaos in my mind had transformed me into an angry teenager. It took many more years to get closer to Hawa again. Our relationship improved when I completed my West African Secondary School Certificate Examination in Freetown and returned to Guinea for a visit. Hawa had completed her International Rescue Committee scholarship in Conakry and was working for GIZ – the German Society for International Cooperation.

I spent weeks catching up and bonding with Hawa. Whenever I visited her at the office, we laughed at a particular walkie-talkie radio communication code: `Tango, six, quart-quart`! Somehow this simple transmission signal code was hilarious to the both of us. Years later Hawa and I were still making `Tango, six, quart-quart` jokes. I think it was the manner in which people said the code to impress those around them. There were no cell-phones at the time, so aid agencies communicated via walkie-talkie. Some satellite phones were available at the head offices of major organizations such as the United Nations, United Nations High Commissioner for Refugees, and the World Food Programme. A rebel invasion of two major prefectures in Guinea – Macenta and Gueckedou - where Liberian and Sierra Leonean refugees had settled made Kissidougou a new headquarter town for aid agencies. Many refugees were resettled to a camp called Kountaya – and Kissidougou was the nearest major town.

Hawa was happy in Kissidougou where she was working with many of her former classmates from the Gueckedou and Fangamandou refugee schools. Most of the students who obtained the International Rescue Committee scholarship with her to study at various vocational or tertiary institutions in Conakry were also working for aid agencies in Kissidougou. My mother lived in the Kountaya refugee camp at the time, working as head of a technical skills training institute for refugees. Hawa visited her from time to time. Interestingly, and perhaps my mother was more discreet than many other Sierra Leonean parents, I never heard her pester Hawa about getting married. As a Catholic mother, she never encouraged Hawa's out-of-wedlock relationship with Augustine, but she never discouraged it either. Augustine was serious in school and a respectful young man – that was enough for my mother.

IV

After my phone conversation with Hawa, I went back to sleep, like a normal college student who is woken up by an early morning call. I will refrain from stating what is considered early for undergraduate students — US college socialites know what I mean. My siblings never even bothered to check the time difference or day of the week. Monday mornings were alright, but Saturday mornings were definitely not cool. However, whenever the country code read 224, 231 or 232, I couldn't resist. I pretended to be awake, even if I had just jumped out of bed to answer the call. I was a light sleeper in those days and the minutest sound or shadow woke me up. A few years ago, international calls were expensive and not everyone could afford more than a five-minute call, but the availability of `WhatsApp` to cousins, nieces, and nephews has made international communication inexpensive.

"Did I wake you up?" The caller asks, not with remorse, but merely to start a conversation.

My relatives didn't really care whether I was asleep, because if only they took a minute to calculate the time difference, they would have realized that no one is up at 3:00 waiting for non-scheduled calls. But I was far from home, so I often felt a strong desire to answer. I always feared it might be bad news when I was called at such odd hours, so you can imagine the irritation I felt when the caller said, "no, nothing, I just called." Well, I thought to myself, it would have been nice if you had just waited a few more hours to call. When I sometimes ignored calls, there were the persistent callers, who, even after leaving voice messages, continued to call. The agony of it all was that some of my folks just didn't understand why it was wrong to keep calling. These repeated calls irritated some of my American friends, but I never got mad. I assume people mean well; they just don't know any better.

I did not always share my African problems with my American friends. My college mates would not have understood why I was responsible for the school fees of relatives, why an extended uncle called me for his rent, why an old high school classmate called me for financial assistance, so I kept these issues to myself as we studied and partied together. The only other person who heard about Hawa's wedding dress request was Prof. Michael Marx, my academic adviser and mentor at Skidmore. He was privy to my odd family news. Prof. Marx had heard many weird stories from me, but even he was flabbergasted by Hawa's request. After patiently listening to the story leading to the request, he shifted in his chair and asked in the kind, but puzzled voice I heard so many times: "Isn't this whole wedding dress stuff a serious delight for women; why would your sister entrust you with this?" With this question I realized Prof. Marx was using a western lens to interpret an African situation. Hawa trusted me a whole lot, but what really mattered in this situation was that she needed a wedding dress from the US where her brother was residing at the time.

I spared him the details and cunningly diverted the conversation to my classwork. Prof. Marx knew when I was evading a question, and he often allowed me to move on. I had no more conversation about Hawa's wedding dress until it came back to haunt me. The situation almost propelled me from the coolest brother to the worst person ever — in the eyes of Hawa at least. Every time I think of that near miss, or near hit, as the American comedian George Carlin would prefer, I still get heebie-jeebies. My siblings regard me as a conscientious person who keeps his promises, but that wedding dress affair still makes me feel like the most foolish person in the world. How did I underestimate the faith my sister placed in me to purchase her wedding dress? I had maintained a reputation in the family for trustworthiness, but I exhibited carelessness at a moment when my reputation needed upholding.

V

Months passed and I had forgotten my sister's wedding dress and moved on with "college life." College life in the US means parties, but I was also involved in many intellectual engagements, or what college ought to be. Around December 22nd Hawa called to follow up on her wedding dress request. She knew my semester had ended and I was about to head home. She had completed all other arrangements and the wedding dress was the only remaining piece. She wanted me to email pictures or describe the dress to her. How does one tell a girl who is getting married in a few days that her clumsy brother forgot about her wedding dress? I had no backup story, so I lied.

I told Hawa her wedding dress was ready but it needed a little fixing. I asked for her size, again, pretending to verify what I already had. I had totally forgotten the units she provided when she told me to purchase her dress. I hate lying, but there was one thing I was not going to do on the phone: tell my sister I had forgotten about her wedding dress. Hawa was excited when she heard that I had already gotten the dress, but for the little alteration it needed. She provided her measurements again. They were either in French or British units; either way I didn't understand any of it. My mother is a seamstress and as a boy I used to help in her tailor shop, but while I ironed, wrote lesson plans, and sometimes even sewed on her singer machine, I never used a measuring tape for any meaningful purpose. My only help when my mother was taking a measurement was to write down numbers as she said them out loud while still holding a measuring tape to someone's waist, chest or thigh.

I was shivering, my heart was pounding, when I got off the phone with Hawa. She must have told her friends that her wedding dress was coming from the US, so I understood the consequence of not delivering. It would have gone beyond being a horrible brother; it would have been majorly disappointing. I was unwilling to assume such a risk, because I love my sister and I did not want to disappoint her, especially for her wedding - no one should receive such a disappointment. Forgotten birthdays are pardonable infractions in a friendship, but a missed wedding is not easily forgivable. Birthdays come and go; we hope marriages last forever.

When I regained my composure and returned to my reality that was college, I went to the dining hall to eat. The whole stress reminded me that I had forgotten to eat lunch. In my senior year, I went through a phase of apple diet, which made me forget real meals. Back then I had the tendency to make whatever I liked my breakfast, lunch, and dinner. I fell in love with baby carrots in my freshman year and stuck to that for a while. One of my friends, Veronica, once watched me devour a bowl of baby carrots and suggested that I would turn orange from eating so much of it. I took one look at my arm and replied that I was safe. She understood what I meant and smiled. My skin is too dark for me to worry about turning orange.

I ate my food quickly and returned to my room to create a plan for getting my sister a wedding dress. I don't give up easily, so the whole situation was not yet code red. I could have reprimanded myself for such clumsiness, but I had no time to self-remand when I still had the opportunity to make things right – or so I thought. I remained calm and started with the obvious: Google. Actually, Google was my only choice. I could not think of any other initial approach besides that ultimate universe of knowledge and direction provided by the invisible genius inside the internet.

I googled, "Bridal stores in Saratoga Springs," and there it was: David's Bridal, Wilton Mall. I picked up my debit card and headed straight for the school bus that went between campus and the mall. It was a snowy day. While every other student on the bus was either drunk or hungover, I was cold, calm, and collected, even though my heart was perturbed. I kept thinking that I was simply going to pick up a nice dress, pay the kind of money I didn't want to pay, and return to campus. The students on my bus, mostly freshmen who had completed their exams and were waiting to go home, were oblivious to the herculean task tormenting me. They shared funny stories of their party night and made fun of each other — who made out with whom, mostly. I tried to be inconspicuous and smiled when a familiar student looked my way. A few of them were residents of McClellan Hall and I was their Residential Assistant – I was the big brother who took care of them away from home. And as a good big brother sometimes should, I ignored their conversations.

As a Residential Assistant, I was guided by the same biblical principle I use as an older brother, "For there is not a just man upon earth who doeth good and sinneth not...take no heed unto words that are spoken, lest thou hear thy servant curse thee." A Residential Assistant can go from hero to asshole in an instant. One is a hero when one lets a student into a building when he can't find his keys, but an asshole when one confiscates booze from an underage student. I disagreed with the 21-year drinking age, especially when most students had already been drinking in high school, but my role was to enforce rules set by authorities beyond our campus existence. I still remember when my high school faculty in Norway wanted to change alcohol rules because students were drinking to an extent that the authorities perceived as "excessive" on weekends, and my Nordic classmates informed our faculty that any such restrictions beyond existing laws would be against Nordic democracy.

I was delighted to see the mall. The mall – a meal that keeps America's consumer appetite wanting more. It was the end of December, so the crowd was beyond normal. Folks filed in to purchase holiday gifts that would sooner or later end up in dumpsters. There were Christmas lights everywhere, and outside the Mall, an infantry of the Salvation Army, in their red coats and Santa hats, maintained a chiming rhythm to their fundraising for the poor and needy. One feels like a horrible human being walking by without dropping a dollar. I am sure that is not their intent, but that is how I felt whenever I passed by their volunteers without giving alms. Ironically, though, it was a rejection of the word "volunteer" that led their founder, William Booth, to suggest the use of "Salvation." An earlier report about their work had referred to them as a "Volunteer Army." Mr. Booth felt they were better described as a "Salvation Army." This Christian Mission is present in 130 countries around the world, saving souls and helping the needy. I am proud of the Salvation Army, but it was not why I was at the mall.

I made my way through the slush of accumulating snow. I was warmer now, but my fingers were freezing as always, no matter how thick my gloves were. I walked through the door as the Salvation Army infantry intently rang its bell. As someone who is regularly fundraising for one charitable cause or another in my country, I commend their courage, but I was not at the mall for charity. My mission was to save a bride in Guinea. I passed through a battalion of people doing their Christmas shopping as I went up and down the aisle looking for David's Bridal. I eventually came to a store space that should have been David's Bridal, but alas, instead of perfectly bodied mannequins wearing pristine wedding dresses, the store was naked. It had packed its belongings and vacated Wilton Mall. The devil knows how to dance on one's grave. I was disappointed and a little scared. The reality of the possible damage that would result from failing to get the dress had not yet sunk in because of the glimmer of hope provided by the option of picking one up at a nearby David's Bridal, but when that possibility was shattered, fear kicked in. It would be a huge disaster to return home just days before my sister's wedding without a wedding dress.

I walked out of the mall dejected. I had no energy to smile back at the Salvation Army infantry at the door. I had difficulty walking to the bus stop. It had become a little chaotic as cars and cart-carrying people began to miscommunicate. Some wanted to ride their overloaded carts all the way to their vehicles while others competed for parking space in front of the mall. Cars usually don't honk in small town Saratoga Springs, but here on a slushy winter, Christmas shopping night, they honked for each other to get out of the way, popping a few angry words out of their car windows. I quietly avoided their chaos and walked to the bus stop where I waited for the bus to take me back to campus. It was dinner time when I got back. Campus was quieter.

More students had finished their exams or papers that afternoon and gone home. I was anxious and hungry, so I went to the dining hall.

VI

I fell in love with the Skidmore College Campus from the day I arrived in September 2004. On a snowy or rainy day, one could use a covered pathway from the student dorms in the South Quad to the library. The covered walkway did not eliminate the winter cold, but it saved us from walking on snow, in the rain, or falling on ice.

After dinner, I recommenced my Google search and located another David's Bridal in Albany, 40 minutes from Saratoga Springs. This was good, yet not such great news for my situation. I do not drive. By December 21st, the Skidmore campus is like a graveyard – dead quiet. Winter break is short, so students rush home to make the most of it. My closest friends had gone home, and two of my best friends, Peter and Amanda, were leaving the following morning. Had they been driving, I would have asked them to take me to Albany first, but they were flying to California.

Just when the agony was consuming the best of me, I remembered an old minivan. It belonged to my dear friend, Alicia Wells, who was still on campus. I was a Residential Assistant on the 2nd floor of McClellan and Alicia was a House Counsellor on the 3rd floor. We were the two staff members still on campus to close the building after students had gone home. We were both assigned the role for practical reasons. Alicia had a presentation on the last day of finals and my flight was on the 23rd of December. We were going to be on campus, anyway. "Are you free tomorrow, Wells?" I texted.

"Yeah, why?" Alicia replied.

"Would you be able to drive me to David's Bridal in Albany tomorrow morning?"

I don't remember what her response was, but I believe it was something with multiple exclamation marks. I couldn't blame the girl, though. How many times has anyone met a college boy who wants a ride not to the liquor store, but to a bridal store!

With the amount of snow in Saratoga Springs that morning, even the three wise men would have changed their minds about road tripping - in their infinite wisdom of course. But mine was an urgent matter and Alicia was willing to drive. Well, not before we spent at least half an hour digging her minivan out of the snow. As you might imagine, I was digging so hard even miners would have envied my skills. Alicia didn't drive around much. Her van was parked right outside McClellan, but the folks in facilities had either gone home for Christmas or were simply in no rush to clear snow because most of the students had gone home. In any event, if snow was my only obstacle, then I had none. I dug.

Before we left that morning, I asked Alicia whether she was certain her exam was in the afternoon. "Yes," she replied.

Alicia had a final presentation for an English class taught by my advisor, Prof. Marx. I had the feeling her presentation was due that morning. I might have gotten the idea from Amanda, who was also in the class, or from my advisor during one of our meetings. But Alicia was sure her presentation was in the afternoon. I was not going to argue with the girl who was about to save me from the greatest sibling disaster.

I was delighted when I saw a sign on a warehouse that read "David's Bridal," but that was only the beginning of act two of my drama. As Alicia and I approached the store, I could see the smiles of the employees broaden. Here was a cute, young, interracial couple! In retrospect, we were a picture-perfect couple. Alicia is a beautiful Caucasian woman and I ain't such a bad looking African, either. There are still towns in the US where we would have been treated with disdain, but we were in Albany, New York.

"Congratulations," said one, then another, and so on and so forth. Alicia began to blush.

She quickly issued a disclaimer: "I'm not getting married!" But that did not help me, because it implied I was getting married, and the ladies assumed the next possible scenario. Before they could say anything, I issued my own disclaimer. I could see they were struggling not to ask the obvious – whether I was gay.

Another 21st century liberal stereotype of homosexual men – getting accompanied by their "girlfriends."

"Oh, well who is getting married?" One of the women asked, disappointed.

"His sister," said Alicia.

"Oh my god, when is she coming to try the dress?" I was beginning to wonder whether all the sales women were on some sort of happy drug at 10:00. I started giggling at the whole situation. Alicia was more composed, so I let her be the messenger of all things strange and shocking. "She won't be coming here."

"Why?" One of the women seemed so disappointed one would have thought her wedding got called off. I realized then that I was really engaged in a prized enterprise for brides. She was not faking – part of the fun of getting married is showing up and trying clothes on. She waited anxiously to hear the reason the bride was forgoing this part of her wedding.

"Because she is in Africa!" Alicia blurted it without remorse, not a hint of regret in her voice. She enjoyed revealing the absurdity of our errand.

Alicia was enjoying the morbid pleasure of gradually unwrapping the weird story behind our presence at the store, in place of my sister, the bride. If everything was weird, the information that Hawa was in Africa and won't be coming to the store was a shock. The sales woman paused, moved her eyeballs from side to side; she looked at me, then at Alicia, then back at me. She might have been trying not to use all the foul languages possible at that moment. She was certainly dumbfounded, and we were amused by her facial expressions.

"So what's her size, then?" She decided to work with whatever we were offering.

I produced the piece of paper on which I had scribbled those units of possible human sizes – that human being my sister – who I hadn't seen in almost a couple of years. Of course, the sales woman didn't understand anything on the paper. I hadn't understood either.

Since I didn't have an accurate measurement or a humanly comprehensible size estimate, it wouldn't have been possible to order a dress even if it could be sewn in a day. The women informed me that David's Bridal usually takes orders and provides custom tailored wedding dresses. However, and fortunately for me, they had some readymade wedding dresses in store. Unfortunately, though, without measurements they were very concerned about the tailoring. Alicia assured them that my mother is a seamstress so she could alter any dress when I got to Guinea. Whether that was possible or not given the time frame was another story, but I wasn't about to mention any more impediments.

One of the women said that since mine was a rather peculiar situation, to say the least, they would allow me to walk through the store and pick a wedding dress from the rack. The only major duty left was to imagine what Hawa possibly looked like since I last saw her. Before embarking on the exercise of dress shopping in the warehouse, I asked Alicia one more time whether she was certain her presentation wasn't in the morning. It kept coming to mind. This time she was a little irritated by my lack of faith, so she called one of her classmates to inquire about the exam – I reckoned just to give me a reason to stop asking.

The exam was already over. I did not enjoy being right. In fact, being right was disconcerting. Alicia panicked. My only consolation for her was to assure her as best I could that I'd do my part to ensure that the absence did not adversely affect her marks. Prof. Marx already knew about my wedding dress saga.

I had faith that he would be lenient with whoever aided me in the matter. The class presentation was only an opportunity for students to share their final projects and learn from each other's work – they had already completed most of the grading requirements by doing the projects. Alicia believed me, but it would not be the end of her troubles that morning. Her phone rang. It was her mother. "What are you up to?" Her mother asked.

"I'm at David's Bridal with Joe?"

"Is there something I should know?" Her puzzled mother asked, jokingly.

Imagine your daughter or sister telling you for the first time that she is at a bridal store when she should be finishing her exams and coming home for Christmas. Alicia turned to me after the call and said, "that was my mom." She was smiling, her single dimple appearing dipper on her right cheek. "What did she say?" I asked.

"We could have given them a little heads-up." Alicia conveyed her mother's response, laughing. She gave her mother an explanation of our incredible friendship and the emergency situation that had led her to drive on snow to a bridal store. I knew it was only one more bizarre story among the many she had already conveyed about her eccentric Sierra Leonean friend.

Whenever I said or did something that was not typically American, I asked Alicia whether it was weird. She was always kind, but honest, when it was indeed weird: "Yeah, sort of, friend."

She often accompanied this response with laughter to assure me that something I did was weird, but funny.

We continued our walk around the store looking at various dresses with a very enthusiastic sales woman leading the tour. At one point we came across a beautiful young bride and her bridesmaids trying dresses. The sales woman said something like, "that's how it's usually done." But I was already distracted by the beauty of the bride. I turned to Alicia and commented that the bride looked like a princess. Alicia must have thought my silliness was distracting to our current mission, so she quickly pulled me away.

"She is here because she is already taken, Joe." Alicia said as she jokingly pulled me along.

The sales woman suggested the prom dress section if we were unsuccessful finding a fitting wedding dress. I was appraising every dress she suggested while trying to mentally picture my sister. "Had Hawa grown horizontally or vertically since I last saw her?" "Was she lenient with her `jollof` rice or has she been over-gratifying with her provisions?" I decided it was safer to assume the larger end of the scale so as to leave room for possible alteration. This was the last time I called my sister "fat."

After almost an hour of walking around the large room of prom and wedding dresses, `et viola`! I found one I deemed fitting for Hawa. She wanted a dress with a long, floating train that could spread from the entrance of a cathedral to the altar. No joke! The train was the only part of the description I remembered because she had mentioned it so many times during our conversations about the dress. My pick might not have been exactly as long as she probably imagined, but it was the longest I found instore that day. Many American women no longer marry in Victorian gowns that require a battalion of bridesmaids to carry from a distance a gazillion miles behind the bride. But this is what makes many African weddings the stuff of legend – other women will talk about the wedding dress for months.

"I'll pay for that one!"

I think the sales woman was taken aback by my sudden resolve.

She wanted to make sure I wasn't taking my duty too frivolously. I had the (mis)fortune of being put into this position by a lovely sister, but the sales lady knew wedding dresses are not matters to be taken lightly. She was already baffled by the fact that my sister had entrusted me with such a delicate responsibility, but she wanted to make sure that whether that confidence was misplaced or not, it didn't turn out to be a regrettable one. She was basically telling me to assume the role, to put myself in my sister's place, to realize that any mistake could be perilous to my sister's wedding. Little did the sales woman know that I knew I would have been better off disappointing the deities than the girl I was shopping for that day. I was determined to get her a dress, not just any dress, but one that would demonstrate my love for her, and my commitment to doing that one major act for her – even if that commitment came late.

When the sales woman brought down the dress and I confirmed my choice, I assumed the only remaining errand was to pay for it. It had a hefty price tag, but the privilege of worrying about cost was long gone. I had already pledged my years' worth of work-study funds. I took a final look at the dress and was indeed assured and satisfied that my sister would love it. I frowned at the price, but quickly bashed myself for such "foolish" thoughts. As a matter of fact, the sales woman had other plans for me.

"Now, let's look for a matching veil." She reminded me that she was the boss when it came to bridal stuff.

"Oh yes, that." I pretended to know what I had come to do.

The veil was easier to find. I simply needed a demonstration of how it was going to stick to my sister's face. Had I given a thought to the obvious method she would use to demonstrate the veil part, I would not have asked. Naturally, even before Alicia could consent, the sales woman pulled her over and transformed her into a bride. Alicia's face was so red it could have stained the veil. I found it rather cute that she was blushing. She was not very amused, but Alicia is always a good sport.

If the veil was an obvious bridal prop, what I came to know as a crinoline, was not. It took both the sales woman and Alicia some patience to explain the necessity of the correct undergarments. In the end, I gave up and basically told the sales woman to just add any other necessary prop to my tab. I had the dress in hand and I was done with the little ornamental details. Once everything was tallied, I decided the bride would need a proper dress when she eventually got out of that sophisticated bridal gown. I selected prom dresses for the bridesmaids, Amie and my cousin Watta. For Hawa, I was captivated by a beautiful mahogany dress, and for Amie and Watta, I got lime dresses. I always bought the same items for Amie and Watta to avoid disputes over whose is better. It is just one of those things experience in the sibling academy taught me.

My wedding shopping spree was over! I emptied my bank account to the amusement and admiration of the women in the store. I was crowned the "coolest" brother in the world for a moment. I even got a phone number out of that whole fiasco, but I never called. I think it was just a customer service number. I still wonder how customer service in Albany was going to solve a wardrobe problem all the way in West Africa.

VII

It was still snowing when we finished shopping. My bank account was empty, but I was satisfied with what I had done. Hawa had a wedding dress I believed would make her happy. When we drove to Albany, I wasn't sure the bridal store would be there. My experience at Wilton Mall had taught me not to be too confident even when a Google search offers hope. I could see that Alicia was still marvelling at the whole situation, but we had a new mission to accomplish. Our next major task was to make sure she didn't flunk her class for failure to submit her project.

We planned our explanation for Prof. Marx as we drove back to campus. The drive back was slow because of the snow. When we got back to campus, I took the wedding stuff to my dorm room, and we rushed to the English Department, where Prof. Marx's office was located. Alicia carried her final project, a scrapbook, in hand.

Alicia and I were now accomplices in a multidimensional tale. She didn't appear too worried. The worst case scenario would have been a grade deduction. Whatever the outcome, I knew Prof. Marx was not the sort of professor that was interested in disproportionate punishments for minor infractions. He is a teacher – not a warden.

When we arrived, Prof. Marx was not in his office. Our worry was about to return. But I had his home number, so I called. His wife, Prof. Catherine Golden, told me that he was attending a meeting in a room near his office. Alicia and I stood by the door, saying nothing to each other, until the meeting was over.

When Prof. Marx walked out, we immediately rushed towards him. He already knew why we were waiting. He must have noticed that Alicia was not in class for her presentation. Our only plan was to state the reason why Alicia had missed her presentation.

We told the whole story and I think Professor Marx was fascinated and amused. He took Alicia's scrapbook and wished us happy holidays. I called my sister to inform her that her wedding dress was fitted and ready. She screamed with joy. I could feel her joy across the phone line. This time I was not lying. I was actually in possession of a beautiful white dress. I thought it was beautiful and she trusted me. I placed the wedding dress in one of my suitcases and there was no room left for anything else. I still held doubts that it would fit Hawa, but I was satisfied with it. Even Alicia said the dress was pretty, but I was not sure whether she was only being a supportive friend – after all, she had seen my distress when I thought I might not be able to obtain a wedding dress. Supportive friends usually do not make fair judges. I have been one of those unfair judges on many occasions to keep friends calm.

I could see that Alicia had also enjoyed the process. In the end, it was an adventure. We even thought it could qualify for a reality TV show we would watch. I wished Alicia could have come with me to Sierra Leone. We would have whispered silly things, laughed throughout the wedding ceremony, and drank most of the beers afterwards – well I would have done much of the drinking and Alicia would have made fun of me.

VIII

I had disaster on my mind from the moment I found out that David's Bridal at Wilton Mall was closed, but it turned out to be an adventurous morning with Alicia. I enjoyed shopping with her. We had never had the opportunity to bond that way. Alicia was not a hardcore partier, so we were often either talking about homework, Residential Life, or whatever shenanigan I had been up to. She is not the kind of person to help a friend halfway. Throughout our time at David's Bridal, she was committed to making sure that we found a proper wedding dress for Hawa.

When everything was settled and we were sure Alicia was not going to fail her class, I remembered that the woman in the bridal store had told me that I needed to purchase white stockings for the bride, which wasn't available at their store. I knew those would be available at Walmart where I could go by bus, so I didn't ask Alicia to take me. She had already helped me majorly. I could handle the rest. I believe one should not use the generosity of one's friends to a point where they are left with no choice but to say no.

I assumed stocking shopping was a task as minuscule as the thing itself. Little did I know that a new adventure awaited me. I had gone to Wilton Mall the day before and that was chaos, but Walmart was a whole different ball game. Walmart, the very emblem of American consumerism, is not where any non-capitalist consumer should find himself a few days before Christmas. Men, women and children were everywhere. The elderly versus the young, the very young versus tenderfoots, fat versus lean, we all went shopping. Many Americans go shopping at Christmas, even if just for discounts. Visiting family members follow their hosts shopping to avoid boredom at home or to buy last minute gifts for relatives they were not expecting to see. It is awkward not to have gotten any gift for cousin Bob from California who decided to show up this year.

I don't regularly see American women in stockings, so I never thought it would be on everyone's Christmas must-have list. A crowd of women overtook each other to move closer to the stocking stand. I stood around for a few minutes and walked away. It was impossible to infiltrate the crowd of dedicated shoppers. I walked around the megastore for a while before returning for another attempt. The stocking stand area was empty, but for a few women still making their choices between brown, black or white stockings of various sizes. American capitalism leaves no one behind – no one who can pay. I didn't know my sister's size in stocking either, but I had a strategy. The stockings were organized by size and colour, albeit a chaotic assortment by the time I got there, since shoppers do not generally return items where they found them. I moved with considerable speed and picked one of each size of white and got out of there.

On my way out, I decided to pick up some trinkets and shoes for Amie and Watta. The whole shopping escapade was getting to my head, so I needed to be out of there as quickly as possible. But then again, that was unrealistic given the stretch of every checkout line. I persevered and got to the head of the line. I unveiled my shopping cart of women's stuff. "Many sisters, huh?" The lady at the checkout asked.

"Yeah." I answered.

"Aww, you must be such a wonderful brother to have!" She said with a smile.

I smiled back, but all I thought was, I wish Amie and Watta could hear you. They think I am a crazy *kempumani*, a westerner. Whenever I am home, they make fun of my every action. The truth, though, is that's what I miss when I'm away. We make fun of each other because we love one another.

I picked up my plastic bags and caught a bus back to campus. At this point I was done with shopping. Campus was quiet now. Most students had already gone home. Those of us who were Residential Assistants and House Counsellors checked every room in our buildings to remove contrabands such as booze and hazardous materials left behind by residents. No matter how many times we told students what to do, we still had to enter their rooms and do it for them. We emptied fridges and unplugged portable heaters – some students, like me, were just never warm enough. I always felt weird entering students' rooms when they were not there, but I also knew how much danger we averted by doing those rounds. During holidays, most students leave campus in a rush, and it was necessary to do additional checks, saving dorms from fire or forgotten pets from death.

When our rounds were completed, House Counsellors and Residential Assistants hurried home to be with their families for Christmas. Alicia had to leave too. I was alone, so I drank some beers and packed my two suitcases with little that was mine. I often used my baggage allowance to bring donated clothes and stationery for children in Sierra Leone, but this semester I had a sister waiting to get married, so she was my charitable cause. Those were the days of two free checked bags, one carry-on, and one handbag. Nowadays, airlines would rather one travelled empty handed, especially airlines on African routes. The planes haven't changed much, they just suddenly ran out of free space.

One can still travel with more luggage, though, for a fee.

IX

My journey from the US to Sierra Leone usually started at Albany airport or Rensselaer train station, depending on my connecting flight from New York City to London, Paris or Brussels.

Connecting flights to Europe were usually in the evenings, so Barbara Opitz, the Skidmore International Student Advisor always booked me on a flight from Albany to New York, which I appreciated. I love train rides through the Adirondack, but when traveling from the US to West Africa, it is better to shorten the trip as much as possible.

Even though Albany International Airport is a small airport serving mostly cities in the Northeast and Southeast US, its security check was operated with all the seriousness of a major airport. Albany International Airport was the first place I ever went through a full body scanner. I had already had debates in one of my Law and Society classes pertaining to the question of whether such a scanner was an invasion of privacy, but when I had to step through it, I reckoned those of us on the opposing side had already lost the debate. I still don't understand why I had to take off my shoes to step into a machine that reveals as far as my bones, but I had long accepted that a US airport is not the best place for freedom fighters for fundamental rights, especially not an alien revolutionary like me. I took off my shoes, stepped into the cocoon, spread my legs and arms wide, just as the rather stoic officer ordered.

As I stood with my arms and legs spread out like Leonardo da Vinci's Uomo Vitruviano, I felt quick shots of air before the door reopened and I was cleared to step out. International travellers have learned to accept many forms of intrusion in the fight against terrorism. I had learned to obey and carry on. As a foreign student, I also learned to answer senseless questions with patience. What I never do at any US Port of Entry is elaborate beyond what is a necessary answer to any question. Too much talking can generate more questions.

The flight between Albany and New York was like life in the small towns of upstate New York where familiar neighbours met each other, and as they do on sidewalks or in grocery stores, they jabbered about the lack of sufficient snow for Christmas or where they were headed for the holidays. I fell right asleep – waking only for my small bag of peanuts and a glass of water.

The good part about checking-in at Albany International was that my bags were often checked to my final destination. The disadvantage of taking the train to the airport was that I had to carry multiple suitcases and carry-on luggage, sometimes without a cart. I often arrived at the airline check-in counter dripping with sweat even in the dead of winter. When taking the train, I also had to make sure my bags were not over the weight limit because there would be no one with me at the airport in New York to keep the extra-luggage, which was usually school materials meant for children in Sierra Leone.

I enjoyed spending time at John F. Kennedy International Airport. I arrived early, and with my luggage already checked in, I picked up my boarding pass and headed for the security check, which was far busier than the one in Albany, with a long chain of travellers going through. The Transport Security Administration (TSA) agents went up and down the lines repeating instructions about removing shoes, taking off belts, taking keys and wallets out of pockets, and placing computers and iPads in the trays provided. Shoes were fine until Richard Reid showed up and tried to ignite an explosive hidden in his shoes – a shoe bomb. My hand luggage was often set aside for further searches because I was always carrying computers and other gadgets for my family. Sometimes I was carrying a large sum of money for one charity project or another and that definitely never failed to trigger the attention of screening machine operators.

When I was cleared, ready, and only waiting to fly, I walked idly in the airport, wandering into stores and looking at luxury goods. When I walked up and down the airport I checked whether there were any bridal stores just to know if it would have been possible to purchase Hawa's wedding dress at the airport. I realized as Alicia had said, "people just don't jump out of planes and marry." Gambling on buying a wedding dress at the airport was foolish. I was relieved it didn't come to that.

X

I boarded the plane knowing that my mission to deliver Hawa's wedding dress was under a tight schedule. Since my student visa was still valid, I did not need a transit visa to go through Belgium. I usually avoided going through the UK when possible, because I needed an Airside Transit Visa to go through London even with a valid US student visa. I didn't even qualify for a proper transit visa through the UK – a country from which mine had obtained independence and joined the Commonwealth. As the name implies, an Airside Transit Visa was basically only valid from plane to plane. Among the many visas I have had to apply for in my lifetime this one annoyed me, but it was often the only way I could return to my country from the US.

I love flying intercontinental because it is one of those times when one has nowhere to go even though one is on his way somewhere. Often one has five or six hours in the sky between New York and Europe. In that chunk of time, one may choose from a limited number of activities such as sleep, read, chat with a fellow passenger, listen to music or watch a movie. I like to divide my time between a book, a movie, and sleep. However, I never fall asleep before the meal is served. I usually drink a couple of beers with my meal, watch a movie, read a little and fall asleep.

I flew overnight and arrived in Brussels early in the morning. The security checkpoint in Brussels was empty, which made it okay for me to walk through the screening machine like a zombie, still waking up from an awkward sleep position in my economy class chair. I passed through border security and walked to my gate. I enjoy walking through airports even when I am sleepy. I took a nap at the gate until late morning when other passengers traveling to Freetown, Conakry and Monrovia began to arrive.

Many Sierra Leoneans in the West return home in December to visit family and celebrate Christmas.

Traveling from upstate New York to Freetown in December requires adjustment to two extreme weather conditions. I travelled from cold, snowy New York to hot, dusty Freetown. I stepped out of the plane, still wearing my winter layers, into a hot air filled with dust. I knew what to expect, so I walked my tired body across the tarmac, eliminating one layer after another. We arrived around 17:00 and I went quickly through passport control. I picked up my luggage and went through customs where I was queried about the content of my suitcases. I told the officers that I was a student in the US and the suitcases were my personal belongings. They inspected my student visa and asked for a Christmas gift. I told them I was a student and I had no money. They grudgingly allowed me to leave. Customs officers at Lungi Airport behaved like one owed them, but there was nothing I could offer, because I knew I couldn't get arrested for refusing to provide a Christmas gift at the airport. I was not Santa Claus for airport security.

My younger brother Francis had crossed the estuary between Freetown and Lungi to meet me at the airport. In those days people could enter the arrival waiting hall – relatives waiting for arriving family members, friends, celebrity welcome parties, and thieves hanging around to hustle. Young men pretended to help unsuspecting passengers and disappeared with their hand luggage at the slightest opportunity. They tried to steal from me on many occasions, but I was smarter. I usually showed up with a tough army backpack and pelican cases that made people fear me. They assumed I was a US soldier.

Sierra Leone was still recovering from a decade-long civil war that ended in 2002. The country was poor and in ruin, even though guns were silent. Many young people who had been involved in the war as combatants were now demobilized and without jobs. Some went to the airport for genuine business, but others were there to survive, and sometimes that meant duping people or stealing things.

It was around 19:00 when my brother and I arrived at the Tagrin Ferry Terminal in Lungi. There was a ferry scheduled for 20:00 and we purchased our tickets. Other passengers who arrived on my flight were also waiting to board the ferry to Freetown. These days there are water taxis one could take from Lungi to Freetown at any hour. Even though it is rather expensive for locals, international travellers have no problem paying $40 each way.

Back in the day, the only other means of getting across were open speed boats with questionable motors and wooden canoes. There was also a helicopter, which I would not have taken even if I could afford the $100 each way. I could never trust helicopters in a country where people are so careless about simple things. In June 2007, 22 sport officials, most of them Togolese, were unfortunately killed when one of those helicopters crashed.

The only major problem with the Freetown Ferries was that it hardly ran on schedule. When it was time to depart we were informed that the ferry would not be departing that night. The next ferry to Freetown was at 8:00 the following day. The ferry had no shelter at the terminal so we were all outside. Those who lived in Lungi returned to their homes. The rest of us, especially those who had travelled all day, began to scream and insult the government. In a society where public officials are not accountable to their people, grievances occur in a vacuum. Whenever things go wrong in Sierra Leone, citizens scream at each other. Their legitimate anger is wasted on people with whom they share their victimization. Those who have lived in the West are often angrier because they had left their country of origin and were now residing in systems that were generally accountable to them. That night I chose not to complain or even discuss the ferry cancellation. I had long decided never to fight my fellow citizens for things I expect from my government. I was already working out how to compensate for the time I was wasting so I could get my sister's dress to her in time. My focus was on the things I could do or change.

Francis and I found a little corner by the Police Post and sat down. We surrendered our bodies to mosquitoes and waited through the night. Francis leaned on my luggage and fell asleep. He had always had the ability to fall asleep anywhere. People argued about our situation for hours into the night. I listened intently to keep awake, but I added nothing. I could no longer vent for the sake of venting. I need leaders to be accountable to their people, but I was keenly aware that my society held no such value. Some of us have learned to accept whatever is dealt to us by those who are more powerful or wealthy. Our society is not yet run by leaders, but by people in power exercising their authority – rulers. It is as that wise man of Nigeria, Wole Soyinka has described it, "only in Africa will thieves be regrouping to loot again and the youths whose future is being stolen will be celebrating it…" In many African democracies, people are partially responsible for systems that oppress them.

We spent the night at Tagrin Terminal, serving our blood to mosquitoes. Some of us would later get malaria and die in a country with a shambolic healthcare system. This is an example of why I sometimes say that many deaths in Sierra Leone are state killings. When morning came, we lined up again for the 8:00 ferry. Just as expected, no explanations were given for the sudden cancellation the night before and no apologies were made. Our government makes us understand that nobody owes us anything even when we pay for it. We were even expected to be grateful that there was a ferry that morning. Some people still complain, a lot, but those they complain about live with impunity. Corruption thrives in our society because our leaders are not accountable. Those who ask questions are considered impudent, disloyal, and unpatriotic. We are religious, so when the government fails us, we take it to the lord in prayer. Since God is not the president, mayor, director or principal, we have to wait for a miracle. Our people will easily accept any answer that makes God the reason. God willing, they say, we shall have electricity next year! And we clap.

As the ferry sailed along, I watched my tired brother and felt sorry for him. I was still energized, functioning on adrenaline generated by the thought of getting to my sister in time. I was drenched in stale sweat. I needed a shower as soon as possible. I didn't grumble because I was afraid of sounding like I was better than anyone, even though it would have simply been an expression of my wish to wash – I had just come from icy New York to hot Freetown. There are those who express their discomfort to show that they had evolved to a Western lifestyle, but I was simply hot, sweaty and uncomfortable.

We took a taxi home to my aunt Kadie's place in Aberdeen where Francis had been living when my uncle, who we resided with since we moved to Freetown, left Freetown to reside in Lungi. Aberdeen village is along the Aberdeen-Lumley coast, which is essentially the downtown of Freetown. Everybody was in a Christmas spirit, but I was not concerned with that because for me, Christmas was no longer enough fun without snow. I preferred a Swedish Christmas, with its Lucia festivities and snow. Moreover, most of my old friends had travelled abroad or simply moved on with their lives. I spent some time connecting with my brother and cousins in Freetown. My cousin, Sahr Kendema, who was entering senior secondary school when I left for Norway was now attending Fourah Bay College as well. It was nice to see him and reconnect. In spite of the limited space in my suitcases I managed to pack presents for Francis and a few of my cousins.

They received practical gifts such as computers, phones, or books. I had foreseen that computers and the internet were going to become essential parts of our professional and social lives, so I bought these essential gadgets for my relatives. I created a yahoo email address in the early 2000s that Francis and I shared long before people in my generation of Sierra Leoneans knew about the world wide web.

XI

Boxing Day 2007. I picked up my two suitcases, which were now lighter, and went to the Freetown-Pamlap station in the east of Freetown. I knew how terrible the road between Freetown and Conakry was, so I had already mentally prepared for the tight sitting position and gallops. During the Sierra Leonean civil war rebels deliberately dug many parts of the highway to prevent military vehicles from getting through. The holes they dug expanded during rainy seasons. A road trip from Freetown to Conakry involved bouncing in our seats as the vehicle rose and fell. I had done it so many times that it didn't bother me anymore. During the dry season I would arrive in Conakry covered in dust like a newly harvested potato.

After going through the many checkpoints on the Guinea-Sierra Leone highway, I arrived in Conakry. One still had to give bribes at various checkpoints before passing through. Officers on the Sierra Leone side had become moderate in their demands for bribes, because of a budding anti-corruption campaign, but those on the Guinea side had become bolder – they no longer cared about proper documentation as long as one paid the requested amount. I arrived around 13:00 and went straight to Hamdalye where Mama Yawa and Docteur Sandouno lived. Docteur Sandouno was getting ready for his role of giving Hawa's hand in marriage. He seemed quite excited to walk Hawa down the aisle, in church, even though he was what is referred to as an *Al-Hajj* – a Muslim who has completed the pilgrimage to Mecca.

Religion has never been an issue in my family. Docteur Sandouno was a Muslim and Mama Yawa is a Christian. It is God who matters. Docteur Sandouno even remarried Mama Yawa in the Catholic church as she wished. Their children were free to choose their own faith – which is rare in Guinea. Some of my cousins are Christians and others are Muslims. They observe major religious days in both faiths as a family. When I arrived in Hamdalye Docteur Sandouno was already amusing everyone with how he was going to walk down the aisle with Hawa – pretending to hold her hand under his arm and taking his steps with precision, one foot after another.

Docteur Sandouno wanted me to wait and travel in his vehicle, but I needed to get to Hawa as soon as possible because I was still afraid that the wedding dress needed alteration. I had to be there ahead of time just in case there was an issue with the dress. My uncle Sekou, Docteur Sandouno's younger brother, accompanied me to the bus station where he helped me obtain a bus going directly to Kissidougou. The buses to the *Forestière* region of Guinea often left Conakry in the evenings so they could travel overnight and get to their destinations in the morning. I was familiar with the journey because I had travelled that road many times before. I enjoyed being awake with the driver in the dead of night, listening to local music when other passengers had fallen asleep. Music is clearer in the dead of night. The clean voice of Tiranke Sidime became sweeter on those quiet nights of travel between Conakry and Kissidougou, Gueckedou or Macenter.

When Sekou realized that there was a young lady in the seat next to me, he shook her hand and said, "take a good care of my nephew," in Kissi. The girl, who was also going to Kissidougou, smiled and nodded in agreement. We did not even drive for an hour when the girl who was supposed to take care of me leaned on my shoulder and snored away. After a while, my only choice was to shift in my chair so she could rest properly. She was so comfortable, it was as if we had known each other forever, when we did not even know one another's name. It didn't matter anyway. She slept; I listened to music and thought about my sister's wedding.

Along the highway are towns that only come alive at night. Those who live there sleep during the day and spend the night selling their goods to travellers passing through. Buses stop in these towns so passengers could eat, pray, wash, use restrooms or just stretch. On random occasions a driver would stop his vehicle to take a short nap. While this might have been annoying, it was a responsible thing to do for obvious reasons.

When we reached one of those rest towns, my sleeping caretaker woke up and was suddenly talkative. She insisted on where and what we should eat. I didn't complain. After all, my uncle had entrusted me to her care. She strongly objected to eating rice and `plasas` and recommended beef sandwiches and tea instead. We ordered our sandwiches. We ate as she talked on and on about everything, most of which I did not understand. It was after midnight and I wasn't really in my conversational spirit, but she kept talking. All I did was answer from time to time to assure her that I was listening.

When we were done eating, pissing, washing and praying to our gods, we boarded the bus to continue our journey. Not long after we boarded, my caretaker was comfortable again. This time she avoided my shoulder and went straight for my lap. I had no choice in the matter – plus I was beginning to like her. I am a shy person, but I have a thing for boisterous girls. I reached my hand across her torso to prevent her from sliding off my lap. A few minutes after I placed my hand across her body, she began to snore again. The car stereo played on as we drove into the night.

I looked out the window to watch deem lights in distant valleys and across dark plains. We drove through sleeping towns with random night owls whose presence was only revealed by moving glows from flashlights. When we passed through towns with festivities, drums were heard in the distance. We went through fields lit by fireflies and chanting crickets. I stayed awake because I enjoyed hearing those distant sounds and watching dim lights along the way. I allowed my mind to synchronise the music with the elements I was seeing and hearing. As the bus zoomed, its headlights piercing the dark, stars spread across the sky followed along like a flock of migrating birds. I watched my caretaker sleep like a baby, which added to my inner peace. The hot temperature transported my mind back to upstate New York where they were experiencing the extreme opposite of my current situation. I quietly marvelled at the fact that we were on the same earth with different weather experiences at the same moment. As folks slept around me, I thought of my friends who were going about their day in New York.

We arrived in Kissidougou at 6:00. I was not worried about finding my way around because I speak Kissi and Mandingo – the two major languages of Kissidougou. As the bus pulled into the parking lot, I noticed Hawa on the side. She had not changed very much since the last time I saw her. I wondered whether the dress would fit her. Hawa seemed nervous. Mobile phones were not yet widespread in Guinea as they are now, so even though she knew I was arriving that morning, she did not know on what bus.

She jumped with her hands in the air when I stepped off the bus.

We embraced for a moment. We were happy to see each other after such a long time. She kept smiling and asking me how I was doing. I gave her the same answer each time: "I am fine."

While getting off the Conakry-Kissidougou buses is easy for passengers, it is not always so easy for their luggage, especially when one's luggage ends up under various merchandise. Many passengers traveling that route were traders carrying wholesale goods in order to avoid paying delivery fees to local wholesalers. The buses and other vehicles traveling those roads were often seen leaning to the side because they were overloaded with goods. Mama Yawa advised against traveling on overloaded buses because there was a winding curve on that highway where vehicles often failed and tumbled into the valley. Back in the day most accidents on the Conakry-Kissidougou highway occurred there.

My two suitcases were eventually brought down the bus. When I was about to leave, I shook hands with my caretaker who was still struggling to wake up. I Introduced Hawa to her and said goodbye. She told me that she lived in the Sandouno compound in Kissidougou and I was welcome to visit her. Kissidougou, like most cities in Guinea, does not have street numbers. Cities are divided into `quartiers` and addresses are noted by landmarks. For example, one lives in `Quartier Madina near Garre Voiture`. With a bit of effort, one always finds the location. Nowadays mobile phones allow one to call the other party to meet halfway. I once asked a boy in Lungi, Sierra Leone, where he was born and he said, "by the airport, behind the hospital." Directions like these are familiar to many

Africans. Sierra Leone is a little different from Guinea, though, because most city streets are named and numbered.

We drove back in the direction that we arrived from Conakry for a short instant and arrived at a small compound off the main road where my mother, who had arrived from Kountaya to assist Hawa with her wedding, was eagerly waiting. I have never been as close to my mother as my brother Francis, but I love her. We hadn't seen each other for a long time, so she must have been excited when she heard I was coming for Hawa's wedding. She was standing there, waiting for me, looking as though she had been standing there for ages. I was pleased to see her. She smiled and opened her arms as I stepped out of the taxi. We hugged and I held her for a long time. I was happy to see that my mother was healthy.

When I am away, my mother constantly worries about some imaginary trouble that might happen to me, and I worry about her health. Whenever I call from abroad and someone tells me that she has a fever or whatever else, I do not sleep well until I am assured that she is alright. I get worried when she is running around, engaging in one activity or another, between Sierra Leone, Guinea, and Liberia. Her response to my order to stay in one place is always, "if ar sidom ar go sik," staying in one place will make me fall sick. I also can't stop her from visiting her other children, which means as terrible as some of the roads are between Sierra Leone, Guinea and Liberia, she has to travel.

I gave my mother the trinkets I bought for her and I handed Hawa the suitcase full of bridal stuff. She was already giddy. I wanted her to try the dress immediately. However, a brother should not see his sister in her wedding dress before her wedding. Even a groom is not allowed to see his wife in her wedding dress before their wedding. When I hear a rule like this I wonder who made it and what was the intent. I am of the view that power and money have enormous effects on enduring cultural norms. Our cultural norms and traditions change faster when those with power or money can no longer benefit from them. This is precisely why, for instance, Female Genital Mutilation (FGM) has not been abolished in Sierra Leone. I have met many leaders who believe FGM is abhorrent, but they cannot condemn it, because they will lose power. Consequently, they ignore an anachronistic institution that violates children's rights and hinders the health of women in our society.

Hawa came out of the room after trying on her dresses. I looked at her with querying eyes. I was expecting her to say the dresses were all the wrong sizes and needed alterations. She was busy smiling at me, so I cut the matter short by going to the point:

"`De klos dem du?`" Did the dresses fit?

"`Dem fit gbet!`" They fit perfectly, she answered.

"`Ar well, naim dat!`" Well, that's it! I said with relief and satisfaction.

My sister did not know the troubles I had been through to guarantee her satisfaction. One of my friends often says he is not impressed by those who fail to try because a task is apparently difficult. Success stories are often impressive not because of the success alone, but also because of the hell heroes go through to bring the story to a successful end. This is not to say that hard work always has an immediate pay, but there is often a reward for it; sometimes payment is merely deferred to a later date. I have stated before that a failed attempt is more rewarding than a failure to try.

Nelson Mandela said that "it always seems impossible until it's done." Many of us never reach the full grind of our human grit because we give up too early. When we are confronted by a difficult task, we resign to the perceived weight of it. If offered a novel assignment, we coil to the novelty of it. In many African societies, patriarchal definitions of gender impose limitations not only on women, but also on men, who are often unaware that even a society that creates an imbalanced power structure favouring men limits men by placing them above certain existence. For instance, a man who could have been a great chef cannot even enter a kitchen in a society that assigns that role exclusively to women. A country can never reach its full potential when it denies education to women and bars them from the labour force, thereby placing the development burden of a society on half its labour force. When a society discriminates against any facet of its population, everyone suffers, one way or another.

XII

Hawa was set to marry. Since family members were gathering, I knew that before the end of Hawa's wedding one uncle was going to ask me that inevitable question for unmarried young folks at an African wedding: `so when are we getting invited to your wedding?` It is even worse for young women, especially those who are unmarried college graduates. These are often the times when parents plot arranged marriages between cousins, if one is lucky, or between a young girl and a pot-belly dude as old as her father. When I was a boy in Gueckedou, some of the girls I played with, especially the fula girls, would disappear for a holiday and come back married to an old man who could barely walk upright. I used to feel a certain discomfort every time I came across a little girl I knew now carrying a huge belly and wobbling like Juno. She would never play with us again under a moonlit sky where we shared improvised stories with beautiful choruses and crushed on each other with teenage desires. While we were still boys, they became wives and mothers. These things are still happening in Sierra Leone.

Many years later, and a bit of travel in Europe and the US, I still knew little about romantic relationships. I had had crushes and kissed many girls, but I had not entered any meaningful relationship that could have amounted to an ever-after. In my junior year of college I fell in love with a girl, but after a short period, we decided that we were better off as friends. It was a practical decision and our friendship has endured until now. I loved her back then as much as I love her now, but I could never work out a relationship with her.

Over the years I have thought of the difference between love in a romantic relationship and in friendship, but I remain unable to eloquently explain how I could never work out a romantic relationship with a girl I love. My reading of Elie Wiesel later brought me closer to understanding my feeling of love in friendship. Here is a quote from Wiesel that provides a meaningful explanation of my feelings:

Friendship marks a life even more deeply than love. Love risks degenerating into obsession, friendship is never anything but sharing. It is a friend that you communicate the awakening of a desire, the birth of a vision or a terror, the anguish of seeing the sun disappear or of finding that order and justice are no more.

The roaming question on my mind is, what would life be if one married one's friend? Does romantic love shorten the depth of friendship or deepen it? One could make an inference and say a romantic relationship makes friendship stronger, but can friendship withstand the demands of love? I have found friendship to be more comforting than a romantic relationship. However, I have not yet been in a romantic relationship long enough to be sure. I don't know how my older sister decided to marry, and I absolutely would not have condoned any form of arranged marriage for her, but I had not yet arrived at a point in my life when I could stand in front of anyone and say, I do.

My involvement in Hawa's wedding preparations got me thinking about the fact that she was getting married as a Catholic in Africa. I have opted to skip the debate about Christianity as a residue of colonialism here, for I have already covered that elsewhere. However, I couldn't help but think of monogamy versus polygamy. This debate might not be all that vital, in the scheme of things, but it is relevant to our existence and the universal application of law in Sierra Leone, especially laws that protect women and girls from gender-based violence and exploitation. For instance, while Sierra Leonean law recognizes 18 as the age of majority, it also allows customary marriage below 18 years. So while children under 18 years cannot legally consent, they could get married under customary law with the consent of a parent or guardian. This is how we have indirectly legalized arranged marriage.

Polygamy, especially polygyny, was acceptable in many African societies before the advent of Christianity and its concept of monogamy. A good Frenchman under the French Colonial system of assimilation was one who, including other French prescriptions, embraced monogamy. In Sierra Leone, men who want more wives or an underage girl simply convert to Islam and credit their religion for their polygyny or child marriage.

Some have argued that Africans were polygamist because men needed large families to cultivate more produce, but this cannot be entirely true, especially because in many of these societies, only wealthy men could marry more wives. One was expected to marry many wives only if one could feed and take care of them. A man could not marry another wife if he was not illustrious or could not afford her bride price, which was usually very hefty for a poor man. So while women were expected to contribute to the household, it was not the primary reason men married more wives. Men who needed more labour simply acquired more domestic labourers.

My interest in polygamy and monogamy is not to determine which is better than the other, but rather to discuss what I describe as a "culture of unfaithfulness" in monogamous relationships in Sierra Leone. Since many so-called monogamous partners are quick to condemn polygamy, my question is, between a polygamist and a monogamous spouse with multiple concubines, who is better? In my view, at least a polygamist is honest with himself by spreading his love under oath. A monogamist who cheats breaches his marital contract and lives a life of deceit. He must often hide from each of his multiple lovers and conjure lies to keep them in love with him.

I was not interested in any of these forms of marriages because I was personally thinking of which road to take anytime soon. My thoughts were merely a philosophical reimagination of our post-colonial societies in relation to marriage. My reflection is only a repetition of that existing, controversial question African scholars before me have popped: is monogamy compatible with African culture? Judged only by the current state of monogamous relationships in Sierra Leone, I cannot say it is a situation of one man one wife till death. So, if you ask me, a polygamous man who keeps his oath to his multiple wives garners more respect in my book than a Solomon of a monogamist, especially when he stands with his wife in front of a priest and swears to take his spouse, "to have and to hold from this day forward, for better, for worse, for richer, for poorer, in sickness and in health, to love and to cherish, till death do us part." In a patriarchal system like Sierra Leone, it gets far worse for women after this.

Marriage, as far as I understand it, is like any other contract. It will work only with mutual respect. A breach of contract is a breach of contract, whether it is one's marital oath or an employment contract. Every breach of contract means an undertaking that was not kept. My sister's excitement about her wedding brought these thoughts to my mind. I was beginning to wonder whether I shall ever marry. The idea of a lifetime companion with whom one is simply what one is sounds delightful, but then again, the question must be asked whether love is meant for that kind of existence. These are not the things one thinks out loud at a wedding, but nonetheless, they were on my mind.

Hawa and Augustine love each other, no doubt, and they made individual choices to accept each other until sunset, but we still live in societies where an adolescent girl is told to pack her bundle overnight, and the next day she is the wife of someone she had never known before. These girls know little about life, yet they are forcefully told to give their lives to men who probably disgust them. Another question is whether we can ever love those we do not choose with our own hearts. It seems, though, that love is not the primary concern of arranged marriages. Among some of our ethnic groups, arranged marriage borders on the purchase of a wife – savitude.

In these borderline slave marriages, when a girl runs away from her husband and returns to her family, say as a result of domestic violence, she is punished and returned to her husband like a lost cow in an honest village. In the so-called civilized sections of our society where patriarchy reigns alongside polygamy, women are told to "bear," let go. Women are advised that they were built to endure the pain and suffering inflicted by men. If she already has children, then she will be advised to stay because of her children - so many women have spent years under torturous conditions in the name of maintaining harmony for their children. Her church will tell her to summon the full force of God's transformative power to change her husband, but her husband will return to her with words from the scripture: *wives, submit yourselves unto your husband.*

XIII

I spent my day talking to Hawa as she cooked for us – potato leaves sauce and rice. I wanted to hear everything about her life, which like in my case, had to be squeezed out of her through persistent questioning. She enjoyed her job and was happy to be marrying Augustine. I told her about the wonderful friends I had around the world and she was happy for me. Hawa never brings it up directly, but I know she worries about me. My knowledge of how much Hawa and my mother worry about me keeps me well-behaved when I am away. I wouldn't want to recompense their worries with a bad behavior that could land me in trouble – bad trouble – for good trouble is my name.

Francis, Amie, Mama Yawa, Docteur Sandouno and Watta arrived later that evening. They left Conakry early in the morning with Docteur Sandouno's private vehicle. They arrived long after we were expecting them because they had been in an accident and had had to wait for repairs to the vehicle. The driver fell asleep and the vehicle went off road. Luckily, he reacted quickly to redirect the vehicle, which saved their lives.

Docteur Sandouno was a very meticulous man. He had told the driver to sleep during the day because they were going to travel early in the morning, but the driver took a short nap and perambulated the rest of the day, which almost cost them their lives. Watta narrated the incident for the umpteenth time and I got tired of hearing the details because

I kept imagining what could have happened if he had not regained control of the vehicle. But Watta would not stop, so for a while, I was forced to live through onomatopoeic re-enactments of the accident.

On the morning of the wedding, Hawa had to spend hours at the Saloon, so she could not be at the traditional wedding Docteur Soundouno insisted must happen. Before we were Christians and Muslims, a traditional wedding was the only way people got married, but these days it is often a ceremonial activity before the couple goes for a proper ceremony according to their faith. While Hawa's traditional wedding was only for ceremonial reasons, it is now normal to see couples getting married, in extreme cases, three times: at a courthouse or registry, traditional, and church or mosque.

Docteur Sandouno insisted on a traditional wedding because he believed our ancestors must always sanction things like marriages, naming of children, burial rites, etc. When Augustine's family arrived to officially ask for Hawa's hand in marriage, for it is the hand that one traditionally asks for in marriage, Hawa was doing her makeup at the Saloon. Amie sat in her place for the ceremony. A girl can represent her absent sister at a traditional wedding ceremony. This flexible rule has allowed Sierra Leoneans in the diaspora to marry their spouses at home with the brides' sisters sitting in for the ceremony, though this presents difficulty for spousal visa applications to the US.

Traditional marriages were previously arranged marriages, so the bride would not have known the intentions of the groom until he arrived with his family to "put kola," that is, meet with the bride's parents and pay her bride price. Nowadays these traditional meetings are generally staged activities to entertain family members on both sides. However, this role play is done in the most realistic fashion. Even as Christians or Muslims, consulting the ancestors is always real. One does not use ancient deities as play things, lest they get angry.

Augustine and other male members of his family arrived for the ceremony. The oldest member of the family, Augustine's uncle, politely greeted Docteur Sandouno and his other cousins who had come from various parts of Guinea to support my mother. My mother, Mama Yawa and aunt Fatu sat by the men. Docteur Sandouno returned their greetings and welcomed them with kola nuts and a glass of water. Tradition requires that when a stranger visits one's home, he must be offered kola nuts and water. Back in the day people walked far distances to see each other, so it was polite to first offer the visitor water and snacks.

When Augustine's family accepted our welcome and offer of water and kola nuts, Docteur Sandouno asked what the purpose of their visit was. Augustine's uncle offered another greeting on behalf of those who were only with us in spirit. The traditional wedding was easy to perform because Hawa and Augustine are Mende. Even though my mother and her family are Kissi, the traditional wedding was done according to Mende tradition. It was easy to do because the Kissi and Mende share similar cultures and traditions. The Mende, like the Kissi, believe our ancestors are present with us on occasions such as marriages, childbirth, christening, burial, etc. I learned these things from Mama Jeneba, who used to call on our ancestors before every meal, throwing food and water on the ground. I sometimes remember her words when I am having a meal: *Jé woma fuli, Ké woma fuli*, in mother's light, in father's light. This means we live in the light of our ancestors.

When Augustine's family poured a libation of rum and offered a ball of rice dough with kola nut on top for our ancestors, they stated the reason for their visit in the usual figurative language that referred to the bride as a rose they wished to pick from our garden. When the suitor's family declares that they have seen a beautiful rose in the bride's family garden they wish to pick, the bride's family makes it difficult by presenting every unmarried girl in the household, excluding the actual rose. If the groom rejects any of the girls presented, he must pay a fee to see a new girl. This could go on for as long as there is time and girls to present.

Only a few girls were around and we needed to complete the traditional ceremony as soon as possible, so we presented a handful of girls before Amie was brought in. She was dressed in purple, her head covered with a beautiful white shawl, like a true bride. Amie was shy and nervous, but she had no choice in the matter. Sierra Leonean children usually have no power to opt out of things their parents order them to do. She was carrying a calabash that contained kola nuts and bride price money. It should have included other items like a needle, thread, broom and a mat, but the groom's family didn't have enough time to include them. These items are still symbols of women's subjugation in Sierra Leone. They represent the domestic roles women are expected to play as wives. It was part of a patriarchal design to teach women what is expected of them from the very first day of their marriage. The calabash is a cooking utensil used to wash food or offer drinking water; needle and thread for sewing; a broom for cleaning; a mat for sitting with the children; and the money is what goes to the family for raising their daughter into a good wife. The bundle of kola nuts is tied so tight that untying it becomes a challenge. This, too, is meant to teach the bride patience in marriage. It basically translates into staying the marital course no matter what terror is inflicted on her.

These expectations remain in our societies, but cultures are changing, and individuals are making personal choices to deviate from the expected when it comes to their marital lives. The number of Sierra Leonean men who choose to treat their wives as equals is growing in spite of cultural structures that exist to undermine such relationships. The sight of their sons cooking while their daughters-in-law chill in the background aggravates many Sierra Leonean parents, particularly mothers. One would think that having gone through the semi servitude of their own marital lives, these mothers would be proud of progressive sons who treat their wives as equal partners, but it is usually not the case. This is only understood through the prism of the systemic patriarchal order of our societal structures. When a girl is not a good wife, as in not submissive to her husband or cannot cook and clean, it is her mother who bears the blame of not raising a good girl – so like every authority that is expected to take a fall for the bad performance of a subordinate, she becomes a strict enforcer. This also feeds the idea of the evil mother-in-law who acts like the Inspector-General for the qualifications of a good wife, and whose son, even with his worst inadequacies, is flawless. Her daughter-in-law must treat her son like a king - the way she had dutifully served his father.

Amie sat by Mama Yawa carrying Hawa's calabash. One of the elders offered Islamic blessings in Arabic, which most of us did not understand. Many Catholics no longer pray in Latin, but Sierra Leonean Muslims still pray in Arabic. We have learned to grant these religious folks the benefits of whatever doubts that whatsoever they are saying is indeed from the Koran. Members of both families offered speeches accepting or blessing the union. The groom compensated various members of the bride's family, including her childhood friends, for not leading his wife astray. There was a parcel for the uncles, aunties, brothers, cousins, godparents, etc., including those who were absent. This is all done because the groom is grateful to these people for their roles in the making of his beautiful wife, her good manners and god-fearing nature. These were not exorbitant sums of money – they were mere tokens of appreciation to keep a tradition.

In a proper traditional setting, when everything is settled between the two families and the wedding is sealed, the bride and groom would join well-wishers outside for a celebration of their marriage. They would sit on a mat where they would receive presents and participate in festivities. There would be food, drinks and music, and folks would dance and throw money on the pride and groom. When it was time, the groom would go home where he would wait for his wife. The bride would be escorted by the women of her family. They would dance her to her new home. The husband would receive his wife and the women would leave, still dancing and celebrating the bride.

There were variations to this tradition according to ethnic groups. In some ethnic groups, the bride was expected to be a virgin and there had to be proof of it. To offer a girl in marriage who was not a virgin brought shame to the bride's family - it was a dishonourable thing to do. The girl would be taken back to her family and her bride price returned. In a few cases she could never remarry, and depending on the gravity of the deception, she would be rejected by her family and kicked out of their home. This was why, among some ethnic groups, the women returned to the groom's home early in the morning a day after the wedding - to collect the white cloth on which the bride was deflowered – it was expected to have blood stains – evidence of virgin fertility.

The women would dance with the blood-stained cloth to a river where they would wash the cloth and the bride. The proud husband might even offer a gift in gratitude to the bride's family for keeping her a virgin until marriage. When all doubts about her virginity were cleared, it was time to focus on the next step, which was fertility. The bride must get pregnant as soon as possible. A barren for a wife was an insult. But in all this, the man had nothing to prove, except that he was from a good family and could afford to provide for his wife or wives. He did not have to provide evidence of his virginity or prove that he was fertile. It has always been the woman who has to prove herself worthy of marriage.

My family is above these superficial prescriptions and Hawa had nothing to prove. She had already been residing with Augustine and given birth to two lovely girls, and if there was any pressure at all, it would have come from the Catholic church.

Matrimony is a sacrament, and as devout Catholics, Augustine and Hawa were required to receive the rite. For this reason, my mother would have applied subtle pressure. She used to tell our local priests how we were doing and who was misbehaving. She sometimes took our report cards to the priest when we did well at school and we received congratulatory comments on those occasions. I was proud to receive a kind comment from a local priest. On the other hand, a comment like "mother said you are not listening to her" made me mad at my mother. But we were raised in the Catholic Church and my mother knew the intervention of priests would have an effect on us.

XIV

Hawa's traditional wedding happened quickly. Amie was happy to get out of the role she had played all morning in place of Hawa. She was looking forward to joining her other cousins as bridesmaids in the Catholic ceremony. I got ready for church too. My suitcase had been loaded with wedding dresses and accessories, so I brought very little to wear – a few articles of presentable clothing I had managed to fit into the corner of one of the suitcases.

My sisters and cousins left to join Hawa. My mother and other female family members left too. Augustine and his friends went away to get ready. Francis, who is way more of an extrovert than I am, was one of Augustine's groomsmen. I was on my own, so I got ready and headed for a modest catholic church downtown Kissidougou. I wore a white shirt and a blazer I had received from one of Professor Marx's sons, Emmet or Jesse – I don't remember which one of them. Emmet and Jesse are identical twins, and while I have now learned to distinguish them, I couldn't when we first met. They were still in high school at the time, but they were taller and broader than I was. I inherited a blazer one of them wore when he was younger and my size. It was a perfect fit. It was so comfortable that I wore it for many years. I had picked up khaki pants at Walmart to go with it. It was simple and a proper fit.

I took a taxi to the church where people were already gathering. Outside the church were curious spectators who had gathered to see Hawa in her wedding dress. Friends and family were gradually filling up the pews. As I walked down the aisle towards pews reserved for family, I saw familiar faces smiling at me. Many of the people knew me when we lived in Gueckedou as refugees. Others I had met when I visited Hawa in Kissidougou. Some were smiling because they had last seen me when I was a boy and now they were looking at a young man walking down the aisle. They were proud. As refugees, we were always proud, and perhaps a little envious, when one of us made it out of the camp for a better life abroad.

I smiled back and nodded. I was proud of them too. They had not left and gone to the West like a few of us; they had stayed and persevered, and now some were leaders of the many humanitarian organizations in town. They had studied under impossible conditions, hungry and homeless on many occasions, and struggled for scholarships provided by the International Rescues Committee to study in Conakry, resisted xenophobia, and succeeded. Though many would have still loved to travel to the West, they were no longer hopeless sufferers. They were nicely dressed, carrying the assigned walkie-talkies of their various humanitarian agencies as a small expression of their professional importance. Cell phones were just making an arrival on the scene, so a few carried Nokia phones and suddenly answered calls so everyone could see that they had phones. I was simply happy to see them again, especially those who had been struggling students, the ones whose examinations

I had graded when I helped my uncle Lord Vandy mark his English and Literature papers. Back then, they saw Lord Vandy as a hard teacher because he never dished out undeserved grades, but now they had praises for him and how his English classes were the best preparation for their humanitarian lives.

I sat in a pew close to the altar. I could feel the whispers, eyes and fingers pointing in my direction as those who recognized me tried to help revive the memories of other old acquaintances. I sat quietly and looked straight ahead as invited guests filed into the pews. I had already put on my patient hat because events such as weddings never start on time here, and no one gets mad, because lateness is an accepted part of the fanfare. Lateness has become so vicious that on many occasions it is impossible to start on time. People never expect anything to start on time. I once dressed up to attend a wedding reception that had 15:00 as the start time. Luckily I called a friend before undertaking what would have been a foolish endeavour. My friend jokingly told me that unless I was the one cooking the food for the reception, I should plan on leaving my house no earlier than 18:00. I got there at 18:30 and I was still early. The reception eventually started at 20:00. These things still baffle me, but most people seem alright with them. Those who attend events, including church, at the stipulated time are the awkward ones. I recently attended another event hosted by a close friend and her immediate reaction was, "why are you so early?" Her father, who was nearby, saw my puzzled face and replied on my behalf: "your invitation says 19:00 and it is now 19:15." They were still setting up for the party. I was permitted to start drinking, so I did, with gusto. Punctuality remains a repugnant value around here.

Hawa's wedding ceremony began like a normal Catholic mass. The presiding priests, altar boys and other celebrants processed through the modest, but elegant church, while we stood and sang the opening hymn. When they were gathered around the altar, Augustine, dressed in a black suit and white shirt, and his entourage processed to the altar where they were blessed by the priest. They sat on one side of the altar. When it was time, Docteur Sandouno entered the church with Hawa. She moved slowly, the train of her dress flowing behind like a peacock's tail feathers. It was a beautiful walk down the aisle. Hawa seemed satisfied with her moment. I was satisfied, too. I wished Alicia was there to see the wonderful job we had done.

I had been taking pictures. I was a photographer in high school.

Photography became a hobby when I graduated and went to Norway. I no longer took pictures for money like I did when I was a high school student, but I always carried a camera, should a beautiful moment require a shot. The photographers in Kissidougou were still using films and I had a digital camera at the time. When I was a high school photographer, I witnessed the horror of other photographers mistakenly exposing films of pictures from events they had covered, so I figured there was nothing wrong with my sister having another set of pictures from her wedding. I ended up covering the whole ceremony.

Rumours had already spread that I brought the wedding dress from the US, and I could hear whispers about it in the pews. Among the people I was most proud of that day was Docteur Sandouno, who was so enchanted to walk Hawa down the aisle. While Sierra Leone, Guinea, and Liberia, unlike other countries around the world, had not had significant religious differences, it was still impressive to have this `Al-Hajj` walk a Christian girl to a priest. He stood in front of a priest and offered his niece's hand in marriage. He seemed to want the moment to last forever as he played the role of our father once again.

When the wedding ceremony was over, Hawa and Augustine, accompanied by an escort of bike riders and other vehicles drove around Kissidougou. Hawa's wedding seemed like the most important occasion in Kissidougou for a long time. I went along to take pictures. We went from the church, up and down the main street, to the reception hall. People had already gathered in the hall, some of whom might not have been invited. In those days, unlike what I have recently seen in Guinea and Sierra Leone, wedding invitations were not strictly enforced. One's uninvited neighbours and church members showed up and that was just fine. Nowadays, bouncers are placed at wedding reception entrances to make sure only invited guests are permitted to enter.

Hawa and Augustine arrived at their wedding reception when there was still light outside, so I took a few more shots before they entered the hall. After this, I decided to sit and enjoy the entertainment of their wedding reception, where hilarious family stories of the couple were shared along with fried rice and chicken. I ate a little and drank a copious amount of beer. As I watched the modest event proceed, I sipped on my Tonton Skol and thought about how far we had come as a family, how my mother had done everything to ease our suffering as refugees. I remembered the long agony my mother lived through when we didn't know Hawa's whereabout at the beginning of the Sierra Leonean civil war, when she escaped Sierra Leone with my cousin Jeneba's husband. Jeneba had come to Pendembu to complain to my father about her husband when rebels invaded Sierra Leone and cut off the route between Pendembu and Kenema. After almost a year of worrying, we heard that her husband had escaped with the children and was living in Fangamandou Refugee Camp. Our father died not too long after we entered Guinea as refugees and before reuniting with Hawa. She never saw her father again.

These are things we never talk about, but I often wonder how Hawa and Amie had fared through the years. Amie, too, has little memory of who her father was. We often refrain from speaking about our father when our mother is around. I sat at a different table at Hawa's wedding reception because I knew my mother and her sisters would be crying all night. Their young cousin, Finda Marie, was with them. Finda Marie moved to Gueckedou in 1994 to help my mother take care of us when my father died. She was a playful, lovely young woman, who knew how to help my mother forget about her pain through stories and laughter. Her presence after my father's death saved my mother from loneliness and isolation. I was distressed to hear about Finda Marie's death not too long after Hawa's wedding. She was a beautiful human being who was loyal to her older cousins.

When the wedding reception was over, we were invited to a local club for a party. I was in a sombre mood, reflecting on my sister's life, and how she had gone from my childhood playmate to a married woman. I sipped on more Tonton Skol and caught up with old friends. One of my extended cousins was interested in me, so Amie and Watta connected us. She was beautiful and I was interested too, but there was no way I was going to make that known to Amie or Watta. As much as they seemed excited to make the match, I knew it would only be a matter of time before the poor girl became their sworn enemy, especially if I showed any sign of affection towards her. I eventually danced with my cousin while Amie and Watta giggled and gossiped on the side. It was a pleasant moment as she nervously looked me in the eyes and her nose began to sweat. She had a distinct round face, which centred her nose. I was nervous, too, but I put up a brave face, placed my hands around her small waist as we danced to a beautiful zouk song.

XV

The day after Hawa's wedding we gathered as a family. It was a frenzy as we spoke above and across each other. My cousin with whom I had danced at the reception was also present, and as I had foreseen, she was already on the wrong side of Amie and Watta. They were calling her names like, `La go`, the chick, which was one of their methods of affectionate antagonism. She was nicely dressed and they questioned her intent for looking swanky that morning. "Ah, la go, are you getting married today?" They laughed and high-fived each other. At one point I said something to the effect that my cousin looked elegant, and fueled the laughter. "*Aaa, mais Frèro, apprecie aussi.*" Ah, big bro loves it too. I was happy to see them enjoy themselves at my expense.

I told stories of my college life in America and horrified some of my relatives with vivid descriptions of pride and the New York Pride Parade. We ate leftover food from the wedding and made lots of noise to the chagrin of the adults. Hawa and Augustine arrived to thank everyone for coming to their wedding. Hawa was wearing the **Mahogany** dress I had purchased for her. It was a simple, elegant dress and she looked beautiful in it. I brought out my camera and took a few more pictures of her. It was a pleasant harmattan morning with intense sunlight. We had all bathed in various lotions to protect our skins from the dryness caused by the harmattan breeze.

For what it is worth, weddings have another function that is important to modern society – it brings families together. While ancient societies lived near each other and didn't wander too far, many families are now spread across distant cities in diverse countries. It often takes a life-changing event like a wedding to compel them to make extra efforts like taking days off from work and making distant journeys to a wedding location. It was the first time, in a very long time, I had many extended family members in one place. My mother's sisters and cousins came to support her.

My mother's family, especially her Tolno, Tonguino and Sandouno relatives, were very kind to us when my father died, and they remained supportive throughout our time in Guinea. In the ensuing few days that I spent in Kissidougou, we discussed family issues and caught up on our personal lives. Conflicts occurred and conflicts were resolved; rumours were clarified and new ones spread; older cousins were pressured to get married, and young men were told to make money. My mother and her sisters cried a few times and we made fun of them as we always do when they unexpectedly go from laughter to tears.

As days passed, the crowd dwindled, people returned to their homes somewhere in Guinea or abroad. I held the record for the longest travel to the wedding. Those who knew about my journey with Hawa's wedding dress thanked me before leaving. It was a heavy responsibility and since the wedding I felt a great sense of relief. I had been overwhelmed by my desire to ensure that Hawa was happy with her wedding dress. We grew up during tragic civil wars and lost our father in a refugee camp. I have suffered and survived. As I grow older, I have become committed to the idea of small joyful moments that have the power to override or at least subdue years of agony. My preoccupation in life is not with material things, but with joy and happiness, and these are based on ensuring that I bring some amount of happiness to those around me. The Dalai Lama and Desmond Tutu have repeatedly stated that we are most joyful when we focus on others – this I believe. Hawa was happy with her dress and that made me satisfied and joyful.

Rituals that bring people together for celebrations have the power to heal wounds and activate love and rebirth. Through celebratory rituals we have the power to transcend the agony of the past and embrace new beginnings such as a milestone birthday, marriage, childbirth, etc. Many African societies have always been cognizant of the healing power of union and communion with others. In the eyes of a newborn, we can see a dead grandparent and embrace the idea of rebirth. Parents walking their children down the aisle and giving their hands in marriage can be a ceremonial handing over of a generational baton for social continuity. Marriage is the foundation of a family unit in a crowd of humanity. When humans come together, they can laugh or cry, console or be consoled.

Customs and traditions can either be the beacon of happiness or distress. I have found that societies progress or are constrained by the customs and traditions that govern them. Every society has justifications for its actions or beliefs, whether good or bad, right or wrong. In the end, east and west, north and south, people seek happiness on this finite journey of life, and marriage is one of the elements we share across cultures.

Joseph Kaifala - Biography

Joseph Ben Kaifala ESQ is the founder of Jeneba Project Inc and the founder and Principal of the Center for Memory and Reparations. He is also a Human Rights activist, a Rastafarian and a votary of ahimsa. He speaks six languages.

He was born in Sierra Leone and spent his early childhood in Liberia and Guinea. He later moved to Norway where he studied for the International Baccalaureate (IB) at the Red Cross Nordic United World College before enrolling at Skidmore College in upstate New York.

Joseph was an International Affairs & French Major, with a minor in Law & Society. He holds a Master's degree in International Relations from the Maxwell School at Syracuse University, a Diploma in Intercultural Encounters from the Helsinki Summer School, and a Certificate in Professional French administered by the French Chamber of Commerce.

Joseph was an Applied Human Rights fellow at Vermont Law School, where he completed his JD and Certificate in International & Comparative Law. He is a recipient of the Skidmore College Palamountain Prose Award, Skidmore College Thoroughbred Award, Vermont Law School (SBA) Student Pro Bono Award, a 2013 American Society of International Law Helton fellow, and a member of "Who Is Who Among Students in American Universities &

Colleges" in recognition of outstanding merit and accomplishments as a student at Vermont Law School. Joseph was one of the BBC World Service Outlook Inspirations Fifteen. As the programme described it, these are "people who show us a better side of being human."

In 2021 he became the first Sierra Leonean to receive the Ford Global Fellowship and in 2022 he was selected as the first Sierra Leonean to serve as a West African Writer in Residence at the Library of Africa and the African Diaspora in Ghana.

In 2017, Palewell Press published *Tutu's Rainbow World* – Joseph's poetry collection. His other publications include: *What I Think: Maxims of an African Philosopher*, 2019, *Adamalui: A Survivor's Journey from Civil Wars in Africa to Life in America*, 2018, and *Free Slaves, Freetown, and the Sierra Leonean Civil War (African Histories and Modernities)*, 2017.

Palewell Press

Palewell Press is an independent publisher handling poetry, fiction and non-fiction with a focus on books that foster Justice, Equality and Sustainability. The Editor can be reached on enquiries@palewellpress.co.uk

www.ingramcontent.com/pod-product-compliance
Lightning Source LLC
Chambersburg PA
CBHW050303120526
44590CB00016B/2466